My Unusual Library

A journey through the wormhole and hyperspace of my bookshelf

Zeeshan Mahmud

DEDICATION

To all the friendly librarians of Southern California

CONTENTS

1. License Plate Book

Imagine this. A total Chad- our protagonist - walks into a Vietnamese market (don't ask why? Probably to buy an ao dai or something...) and bumps into a Native American person. He pulls out his cell phone for an unmistakable YouTube glory opportunity, makes some svengali motion with a pocket watch, locket or perhaps plain hand-gestures like a pseudo-David Blaine and then suddenly breaks his silence: *Are you from Choctaw nation?*

Now depending on the gentleman, he might either consider him a total creepo' or a genius. I am sure many of us have fantasized a variation of this scenario like Botvinnik running through a database of his mind countless times. (Of course, in this #metoo era, you do it to a smokin' hot damsel, then brace yourself for some lawsuits. But more on that later...)

What is the secret to our magician's effect? Simple. He memorized all the license plates in the parking lot and found one that gave the clue away as apparently he read the *License Plate Book* by Thomson C. Murray.

As I was flipping through the jaundiced, watermarked, autumn-crisp pages of the book, I could not but think of anyoneelse than Sherlock Holmes. This is sure to be found in his arsenal! I mean in order to pull one of his devious and mischievous 'stunts' he *has* to have mentally photographed the content. Who knows perhaps that was my subliminal intention as well the first time I picked it up from Buena Park Mall's bookstore?

The routine was simple. My mom would hand me an allowance of $15 everyday, which in turn would be funded by my father's hard-earned income in a monthly allotment. The first thing being a terrible addict I would do was wait outside a shady, f-paying-a-license pot dealer's doorsteps sharp at 8 in the morning. I would spend about 8 for a gram and then squeeze out a Redline ($3.28) from a liquor store.

The residue or dross would be 2 dollars. In the afternoon, my mother would gladly hand out another crispy 5. By now I would have about $4 after spending the money on Swishers. This is scraping off the barrel folks! Then I would take her car - I repeat *her* car- and dawdle to the mall. I would burn $2 on the automatic chair-massage leaving me with two dollars even. And this is where the dopamine would soar through roof ladies and gentlemen!

Because constraint matters. If someone were to give me a choice between enacting a daily life of Jezz Bezos on a ritual basis or to live like a penniless-dharma-bum-drivin'-a-2015-CRV, damn right you can guess I would have chosen the latter at that stage of my life. In fact, in my creative memoir *At Will*, that is where I left off in the final musings ie. it is not always about playing the role of a rockstar in this Indra's-Net-Maya-induced reality but rather dawning on the garb of a janitor or a boring 'extra' which somehow gives one *more* meaning in our humdrum existence of life. Call it *yugen* or *aware* if you will.

With 2 dollars to burn and a library of books to choose from, on one such occasion I picked up this gem for a buck or two, my indestruc -tible mind forgets. People often assume one would need a cornucopia or reservoir of never-ending-creative resources to get the synaptic firestorm going. No. Remember MacGyver? Only when you are *forced* to apply unrelated items bringing them into juxtaposition, that the magic occurs.

This continued for a while. I was at the peak of my life. Sure I was smoking pot a lot. But after waking up at 4:00am and doing the whole Jocko Willink/Hal Elrod schtick of meditation, morning run, intention or ikigai, affirmations, gratitude, cold shower, learn new things, positive power posture, Nightingale-Conant audio blast in the morning and top it off with a dab from the shady drug joint, I would literally be limitless and unstoppable. Because my mother gave that paltry allowance and I had to make the best out of it.

Sure she spoiled me to an extent as I constantly found myself broke, but there was a thrill - a different kind of thrill- to reap that *unknown* extra title, book title, from a used book store where they range from a dollar and up. In the immortal words of Bon Jovi, that was the best day of my life.

Almost like a telemetry, all these thoughts and memories came back to me as I started pursuing my old books again today. The book is probably a 1979 print edition and this is a must-have for any creative or unusual library. In fact it was at my bottom shelf under a stack of other books and I had to pull it out since I love the creative niche of it. It is a sui-generis genre. And I hardly doubt anyone can find it in any airport bookshelf or a glitzy retail store.

As for the content? Well it is kind of like a cheiromancy for law enforcement officers where an agent may speak volumes just by a single glance at an offender's license plate. There are tons of nuances, codes, keys and details that one may glean from it. One such factoid that may be etched is a tribal nation's name. Of course since it has been printed a long time ago, many of the format and template might have changed and the knowledge may be obsolete. Further, it also talks about tracing back its owner by filling out a form to DMV. Yeah. Very stalker friendly.

But I doubt if all these are relevant since many of the color codes or other symbols could have changed and the petition to seek out the owner is done via a digital platform. This book itself may not be that resourceful as in modern day and age we can plug our phone and pull out any frightening details about a car sans license plate.

The book is arranged into sections by state and has a fun 'game' part to it as well at the back. For instance, a family might have a ball picking out out-of-state license plates while on a long trip or for that matter make it a goal to spy as many states as possible.

Whether you are a detective - real life that is! - or a law-enforcement officer, this will sure come handy as any knowledge is useful. In fact, I recall (I may be wrong) that Asimov in one of his books mentioned Pliny the Elder (or it could have been Younger..) that all books (*shudder*, the Walmart Amish Romances as well?)... all books have something valuable to offer. This I agree. Whether it be a plot of *Slumdog Millionaire* or if you were to appear on Jeopardy! or make someone spit her drink out like Nardwuar, this book sure will find its way through to the Kurzwelian singularity of Project Gutenberg database for its taste of immortality. And if not for anything, then solely for its lustre of creativity factor.

Oh by the way, to the trained eye a license plate can reveal the identity of a state senator as well!

Sleuth on amigos. (*In my best Pierre Bernard impression*)

2. Levels of Infinity

Carrying us the bus trundled forward down Valley View. A man is seated across me with his fishing pole.

"Cool shoes you got there…," thank god he broke the silence as I didn't have to!

"Thanks," I looked at my white **Pumas**.

"Yeah, I used to have a pair of Nikes. My wife threw them away."

"Haha…" nervously I was being polite. "So you fish?" and finally I blurted out as I was itching - rather dying- to get in his brain nerves and cells regarding fishing to dissect my dewey decimal system in my head.

"Yeah, a couple of perches. That's about it."

"Oh I see.."

"Yeah I mostly catch-and-release. My wife here likes to cook." Then I noticed a hunched-over, typical-California-jolly, at-peace, deified "liberal" old woman working a knitting wool with the focus of solving a Rubik's cube. "Just kidding," he gave her a gentle elbow-rib.

So much for fishing archive! I thought. Then the next sentence from the man showed light:

"Haha I was just kidding. She is actually a professor of maths at Fullerton."

"Oh wow."

"Yeah. She did her PhD in maths from Columbia." The chubby man in safari shorts and hat gave her another hearty glance all the while careful to avoid touching the tip of his pole to the onboarders.

"Oh wow." I said. And then I did the unthinkable in this day and age. I blurted out something from a never-ever-should-in-zillion-years faux pas book. "Yeah not too many women mathematicians are out there."

"Haha, she gets that a lot. Especially at parties."

"Hypatia.. Who else Sophie Germain. Lovelace...," I was completely dialled in. Zoning.

Now the mathematician took notice. She slightly looked up and gave me a look.

"No-ether, or no-'eather'... someone like that I think."

The lady smiled now and finally broke her vow: "Haha yeah as a matter of fact I did my thesis on her."

"Oh really?" I was equally amused.

"But I did not think of it. I mean not consciously as to how many there are. Women mathematicians I mean."

"Yeah… haha. And then there is the Russian I think.. Sovaya.. One Iranian one."

"Haha, you know a lot! Are you sure you didn't major in maths?"

"Haha no," I replied, trying to change the subject "I think Emmy Noether was from Erlangen. Probably that is why the Erlangen program or something."

And then you get off. Off in the mist the mysterious man in Santa-Ana-tattoos and a American-flag Polo t-shirt disappeared. You don't talk about Fano nor his planes or about Grothendieck or about Zariski topology or Cech homology. You just mention those subtly and do the mic drop.

Ok. Snap back to reality. I mean come'on folks. Seriously. What are the odds of it happening? Practically nil that you get on the bus and impress someone with an odd curio you gleaned from reading Hermann Weyl's *Levels of Infinity* edited by Peter Pesic which you might have picked up on some odd, rain-cloudy Wednesday from *Barnes & Noble's* trying to assuage and abate the Kafkaesque winter dreariness or June gloom, who knows!

But there are times you come close to something similar which must be like getting a cocaine rush as I can only imagine. F'instance, when I was doing Uber once I blew away a girl's mind by asking her if she is from Ulaanbaatar once hearing she is from Mongolia. I also told her about a tribal custom of eating BBQ-ed goats that are gruesomely stuffed... (I actually didn't use that term) and she gave me the highest civilian compliment "Wow, you know more about my country than I do".

I was perhaps referring to a documentary I watched on YouTube about *khorkhog* and I just happened to know the capital. There is really nothing under the hood folks. It's all a simple matter of having to know your basics. Such as world capitals which again served me right during another Uber trip. As the friendly lady with her kids said she was going to the Bahamas I blurted out "Where? Nassau?" and she was feignedly impressed, although she revealed it earlier having read my bio where I mentioned I know French.

Such spurious knowledge might give an aura of godly vibe, but it is all gimmicks. No one can know that much. No one possibly can. For instance, even after browsing Weyl's book so many times it was only yesterday I found out that tucked deep in her pages it reads:

> [In the Muslim world during the eight through twelfth centuries, the Mu'tazili *mutakallimun*, the philosophers of *kalam* (meaning speculative theology), argued that not only matter but also space was atomic; see Wolfson 1976 and Pesic 2002, 26-28.]

Of course, you flipped through the pages a thousand times but the simple fact of finding something novel upon being forced to do an electronic-fast and look at the books you hoarded all these years is electric. The enlightening part was that I would have never expected medieval Muslim scholars talking about space being atomic in such a brilliant book.

Going back to the parlor tricks, Uber was not the only place I was doing my blackmagic. Even in college I used to blow people's minds - even though no one explicitly mentioned but the sensation was palpable - when I mentioned *dressage* and *mace* in anthropology class, or for that matter *ouroboros* in Art History. But not every one of those moments where James Bond-y. I mean when asked about the master of Leonardo I slipped and mentioned Vasari (who wrote about the lives) instead of Verrocchio. The professor was polite to correct me and bring me down a peg or two yet assuring me that yes it was "one of the Vs".

Another time after chancing upon a security guard who is from Egypt I mistakenly assumed he would be Muslim. Turned out he is a Coptic and that's when I blabbered on about Baba St. Kerollos as after sighting the church million times upon passing on my way to mom's doctor I finally was forced to Google.

These are not unusual. Something happens. Probably a flood of dopamine or even when you recognize something 'familiar'. For instance, if you happen to know the meaning of *lachrymal* and on your visit to the optometrist you see that term on a warning sticker - say, in the manner of 'with lachrymal pressure' - then the light switch goes off in the brain. These are all theory by the way. I don't want to receive hate mail.

And it did when I went to get the registration sticker attached to the back of our license plate. (Although we have screwdrivers for some reason my mom wanted me to pay a dollar and get it 'professionally done'.) And then when I asked him to draw a line across the sticker with a blade so as to prevent it from being stolen, he off-handedly mentioned how the modern ones might have perforations. "Yeah it is an idea. Someone had to think of the idea." I have yet to see one with perforations, but I wondered if it could be *his* idea. "Yeah I mean just like the guy who had to think of those things your shoelaces to prevent it from being frazzled."

"You mean aglet?"

"Yeah *aglet*. Not too many people know that. Wow. I am pleasantly surprised you know that." Again I felt someone must have stabbed my heart with an injection full of cocaine.

Such impromptu legerdemain are rare but when they do happen,whether you ask the guy, who lives in a van erstwhile being in 'flooring business' during a game of chess, if he knows *parquetry* or say talk about 'buckyballs' in hospital, these give you some rush which no drugs in the world can mimic.

I would have spoken more about the hospital but HIPAA confidentiality prevents me otherwise. Oh look. My how the time has flown. And we haven't even discussed the book!

3. Practical Blacksmithing

This is another of those books which I attempted to memorize cover-to-cover yet didn't read a single word. It was on the discounted section at *Barnes & Noble* and perhaps that is why I bought it, but never got around to figuring it out.

I can only picture taking a *Limitless* pill and scouring my brain for the right information and knowledge from the deep recesses of my subconscious while malleting away on a tempered gridiron mail. Or acquiring a full blown level of mastery from a *Matrix* simulation, for that matter.

But of course the truth is you can read four thousand books on this topic from the Library of Congress and you won't know the first thing about blacksmithing. Such is the iron-y.

Certain fragments pounce right out of the page of M.T Richardson edition. For instance, as I flip the through the pages, my attention is caught of guard by the following:

> Polybius asserts that the Roman soldiers wore chainmail, which is sometimes described as "molli lorica cathena".

Words like *damascening* stands out from the introduction and you even realize no matter how much knowledge in which I must delusionally swim, there is an ocean and abyss of information where I will be floundering such as the fact how iron smithing had ecclessiastical connection such as the grille of Canterbury Cathedral.

Much of the 883-page book is filled with figures of tools with a section on *swage*. I don't know what *swage* is, nor do I want to kill the suspense.

The funny thing is as much as this can niftily be inserted in a collector's edition, it is actually a dry and boring book to begin with. Kind of like the locksmithing book I once read save but the sole fact that anything can be a lock: *for instance, alligators in the moat by a keep*. You have to give it to the creative imagination, I must say.

But no such nuggets in this book. Only hands-on activities I ever did in my life was Woodworking in Pretoria Boys High School, which I morbidly avoided simply because of a pre-millennial fear of getting hurt by a hacksaw as I recall the notice in the workshop of the bald headed teacher, probably Mr Van Wyck, of bulleted lists of conducts not allowed and one of them being "No horsing around".

I also hated the precision needed in the architectural drawings which was a bitch as it was all specific maths and I couldn't bother to invest in grid paper and straight edge.

The next class that gave me phobia was the raku ceremony during Ceramics at OCC. Yeah, that must be the 'closest' I ever got around holding tongs, while the alpha of the crowd, a bearded-hrishi student, completely aced it. He was the one who always raised the 'hand' and was up to any challenges. And the thing about him was he had a face you would see in a Burning Man or Coachella who must just about have had another LSD trip and figured out it would be good to go back to school and try Ceramics to get a taste of the liberal arts. At least that's the serene vibe he emanated. Only thing missing was an orb or halo.

At the back there is an exhaustive list of terminologies in the Index and a Table of Carriage Bolts on the opposite side. There is also something called the Sellers or Franklin Institute System.

While to a layperson all hammers look alike, at one point, the author mentions how a smith may have fifty of them.

No the book did not make me Hephaestus overnight and the procedures of thill coupling doesn't exactly roll off my tongue. But for some reason I felt it more rewarding to play pretend and act like a bank robber about to pull out the latest heist like Robert De Niro in *The Score* studying deeply under a lamp as I was reminded by the plan of a smith's shop or the pictures of early forges.

Perhaps such force of imagination is too good for my own truth as no matter of pretense enabled me to commit to memory the 883-page tome.

I will end on this note. This was not my first rodeo as earlier I tackled far 'easier' material such as Dickens's *Bleak House*. What I found was I couldn't learn by rote an ounce of syllables. Then God revealed His finer gimmicks of life, where as I wanted to get the gist of the whole Jarndyce and Jarndyce, I chanced upon a lady on Youtube whose favorite book it turned out was... *this*.

Then it knocked my socks out when during an interview the host was reciting a passage, the lady effortlessly in one breath finished his sentence.

Such is the power of love and pursuit of knowledge than the pure egoic method of brute force which I unleashed so boorishly to consume the Blacksmith's Bible.

But enuff omphaloskepsis.

4. Special Forces Training

A modern day special forces operative is a Renaissance man. He is the ultimate supersoldier. *L'uomo universale*. Leon Batista Alberti polymath of his generation. Not only he has to know about botanical edibles such as stems and leaves or that barks like "birch, pine, aspen, willows and cottonwoods" can be good source for food, but also the typical mastery in rappelling and quinzee making as well as knowledge of poisonous fungi, night and arctic navigation, astronomy, skijoring, first aid, laws of war along with his FN SCAR STD and other knowledge of weaponry and assault rifles.

That's why I love it. Precisely because... and as the title *The Mammoth Book of Special Forces Training* suggests, it is an encyclopedia. It has a smattering of everything.

From the creativity of Sayeret Matkal to creating tourniquets and possessing knowledge of bracken (*pteridium aquilinum*), it keeps you hooked and browsing. I especially like the fact how Jon E. Lewis somehow equates creativity as a prized skill for the special operatives, because one might mistakenly assume it to be a tome of workout for alpha guerillas.

Speaking of fitness, the training does start in the middle of the book. It asks you to sit on a chair and find your Resting Heart Rate from the start. Spartan. Minimal. And yes easy enough. But slowly it devolves into the unpleasantness of workout schedules. He encourages running along with weightless training and has a section called "How to Run" along with nutrition suggestions.

Everyone's heard of helmet camouflage. But how many are aware that smell can be part of camouflage too? Along with shedding your bad habits, smoking should be one of them. Perfume in your body odor may 'give away' your hideout. Little details like this really make it a perfect read.

For instance, did you know that "box jellyfish and Portuguese men o'war cause the same symptoms [excruciating pain, diarrhea, swelling, vomiting and slow heartbeat] and paralysis of your breathing muscles as well"? Solution is a tight tourniquet between your wound and your heart. *Fish venoms are destroyed by heat and the pain is eased greatly by the application of hot water.* It will resound in my head forever.

Under the vital survival skills such as the "snake bite" treatments we learn the tale of the Texas Farmer. An old farmer in Texas was bitten by the rattlesnakes he reared by four times. Then when later on he lived with Navajos, he was bitten again, they performed a weird ritual. After cutting an onion in half and applying them against the bite, they threw it away as it turned green and repeated until the color showed no more.

Facts such as the following are also neatly tucked: "By walking slowly and resting for 10 minutes every hour, a man in good physical condition can cover between 20 and 30 km (12 and 18 miles per day) if he has sufficient food and water." Realistically it is possible to walk 16 km or 10 miles on a gallon of water. This is why in a given situation night travel is best as you dehydrate less.

Special Forces history dates back to a hospital bed in Cairo as the book suggests. Since the book is heavy and I can keep on going scrutinizing for a while, I recall somewhere having to read where visualization practice such as picturing which way the doorknob turns during UBL raid helped shave off seconds.

See most people like that mental imagery part of the Navy SEALs and what not. As did I. And that is why I miserably failed SEALFIT. Because as the coach decreed: "You need to have a solid foundation first, then we can build on it." All those nifty visualization tricks are just gloss. It will make you the fastest driver on track, but only if you are a lamborghini already.

I can't remember but I might have bought this book and others during my pre-ritual of attempting Kokoro 42 of SEALFIT. Books can only take you so far. But I did learn in Cade Courtley's book how he disassembled and assembled his Chevy or Buick like a LEGO set in his head to kill time while being confined in a box during SERE training. While in *Never Quit*, the dude who was shot in his head, the paratrooper found SERE to be a breeze.

These people are a different breed. You can't take your average Sunday butterfly collector or model train builders and turn them into combat trained supersoldier devils overnight. In some ways, you have to be born for that. It has to be a destiny. Sure the average geek from the street and lepidopterologist with regimen training of 3 to 5 years can turn him into a behemoth machine and a juggernaut, but by then that *is* his way of life.

Hey. If anyone proved it. Then it is Kumail Nanjiani.

Then again there is a limit to a soldier's skillset. I guess in a brash form of challenge before I departed Kokoro all embarrassed, I left a souvenir for the coach. It was a Haniyama mechanical puzzle. While it was a genuine form of gift, it may - as I realized- could be misconstrued for an ego battle. Because you can do a gazillion pushups but you cannot blast your brawn through the solution with explosives and Semtex.

But neither did I know it as well. I was a troll.

However, things are changing. There is an NFL player with fuckin PhD in mathematics from MIT and Jonny Kim is a goddamn Navy SEAL astronaut who has Bachelor of Arts (*summa cum laude*) in mathematics and a received a Doctor of Medicine from Harvard Medical School. I am gubeezeus… where do I even end.

So there are people out there with a deadly amount of knowledge and intelligence out there. You never know one might be standing next to you in a checkout line at a 7-11 store. This is perhaps a great privilege living here in the US and California which opens a doorway and portal to these whiz species who exist in this ecosphere.

Come to think of it I met three Navy SEALS during my whole stay. The third… well, HIPAA confidentiality will rule out as it was during a hospitalization and court visit. But the first one didn't even hide to flaunt. It was on an aikido mat. He was tattooed, shaved and every solid ounce of his flesh was built pound for pound. He told me to choke him. *WTF.* Apparently staying underwater in the cold for so long made his veins "callus".

He was sly too.

"I just had my laundry done, that is why it may be wet." He said during a judo hold session.

"Oh yeah. Sorry. Me too."

There is a thing called esprit d'escalier where you get that 'wit' upon leaving the situation. Well if there was any opposite form of that, I received it as I later drove away from the hotel lobby.

This guy made a moron out of me. Because it was I who had the wet gi.

5. The Shell Collector

Anthony Doerr is a Pulitzer Prize winning author. Needless to say he is a...doer. His photo at the back cover resembles a more Buddhist version of Tim Ferris sans the hairpiece. I picked up his "Shell Collector" from the popular brick-and-mortar store and it tells that he is a fine author. Very poetic.

However, I never got around reading it. It was a bit too fictional for me. Too prosaic. While the lucre of the title was salivating, the content inside lacked the nacre. The cover is fantastic and shows a classic plate of shells with delicious labels in small, cursive font. But what didn't cure the fix was the fact that it didn't deal 'too much' with shells.

Perhaps I was expecting a Sherlock Holmes vibe or a recluse who spends years studying shells in a fossilized attic. About *C.Giga* or any turbinidae. Yes, the same ones which look like the headdresses of shangri-la girls of Thailand, if not Shredder's vehicle in *Ninja Turtles* which drills through ground. (Little know my surprise when it turned out our dear Uncle Phyll of *Fresh Prince* lent the voiceover for the Supervillain). But the book lacked that tangent at all.

It's fictional. The story is 'too perfect' and the writing of the prose is too polished for my taste. Had this book been in the same non-fictional vein as the birdwatching memoir in *To See Every Bird on Earth*, I would have been totally game. Yeah, I am one of those with a strange fetish for non-fiction books where the real life recluse is more bizarre than fiction.

Clifford Pickover's *Strange Brains and Genius* tells of eccentric geniuses and I reckoned it would be in the same vein. Here is an excerpt from Amazon description:

> "The Pigeon Man from Manhattan" Legendary inventor Nikola Tesla had abnormally long thumbs, a peculiar love of pigeons, and a horror of women's pearls.

> "The Worm Man from Devonshire" Forefather of modern electric-circuit design Oliver Heaviside furnished his home with granite blocks and sometimes consumed only milk for days (as did Nikola Tesla and Thomas Edison).

> "The Rabbit-Eater from Lichfield" Renowned scholar Samuel Johnson had so many tics and quirks that some mistook him for an idiot. In fact, his behavior matches modern definitions of obsessive-compulsive disorder and Tourette's syndrome.

The Shell Collector alas! didn't hit the spot. But still I kept it. It is about a blind shell collector stationed in Africa. It contains other stories but the first one is more plot driven. Very Stephen King-y; and I do not like books which are Stephen King-y, or any of the range that covers modern day bookshelves in airports, retail stores, and Walmart. Nay. Not a fan of any mainstream or popular genre be it *Poisonwood Bible*'s author, Grisham, Terry Pratchett, Dean Koonitz et ilk. See, no one explores books that ensconce the weirdities of *Finnegan's Wake* now, or for that matter give a taste of Pickover's excerpt.

Books are written to drone us. They are deliberately written in 8th grade style to appeal to soccer moms and not those DMT-smokin', former computer programming wunderkinds from Caltech who loves collecting unusual totems with a cache full of dirty MILF porn. Nay, the style and substance is watered down.

Come to think of it, the only author of mainstream genre with the glossy, glitzy covers and embossed font whom I really embraced was Robert Ludlum. Eric Van Lustbader gladly killed that saga. This is why you will never see me near the paperback shelves of the contemporary authors, but in awe of titles like *What the Dormouse Said: How the Sixties Counterculture Shaped the Personal Computer Industry*. These book titles spell more imagination than the folklore world of those authors.

The story is around a poisonous species of shell. It passingly mentions *Conus tessulatus*, *Conus obscurus* and *Conus geographus* on page 21. And that's about it. I also don't like books that are written after research such as Dan Brown's one. The strain shows. The only short story I really enjoyed which was written in 'simpleton' English, plot driven and had a subdued and subtle tone was about a blind numismatics expert in some anthology about Victorian detection fiction. See the thing is just like painting realistically is now pretty much obsolete after the invention of the camera, I find that mimicking Austen or Dickens is really a moot skill. No one cares. As SpongeBob points out.

The purpose is not to be anal or nose-stiffened cynic. Or dogged. (See what I did there? Cynic=Dog). It's all subjective, but society favors those authors who ruffle feathers less and are very 'vanilla' and bland in taste all under the guise of 'readability'. *Slumdog Millionaire* had the perfect strike and balance. It had intellectual dint and dosage with just enough gritty realism.

Perhaps the reason why I was so miffed was because I myself wanted to possess an encyclopedic knowledge about shells at one point in my life. I was enthralled by William James Sidis and while his phenomenal brain was a product of nature, I wanted to artificially mimic it and be the *next* 'Good Will Hunting'. Thus I would spend night after night in my security stint fruitlessly trying to memorize minute details as to the sizes in inches, geographical habitat facts and other boring stuff hoping just like Bill Clinton, Sherlock Holmes or any Rhodes Scholar in a Jeffersonian Dinner amaze the audience with my breadth and depth.

I recall the jingles I read in Feluda (Satyajit Ray's version of the detective) or even Holmes who spoke nothing else but x in a dinner table. Even in a James Bond novel which I espied upon but never pored over it, Ian Fleming at one point wrote how Bond would listen to anyone if he is an expert (the expert being that of gold in that particular instance).

It is truly remarkable to be under the auspices of an expert. Once I met a lovely birdwatcher who miraculously summoned unknown species from thin-air from afar, which even after borrowing his powerful scope, I could not spot. And it doesn't have to be expertise in some all encompassing topic.

Just the other day, I found a YouTube video upon searching "How to Go Down Internet's Rabbit Hole" about a guy who seems to have devoured all the tutorials on beard trimming and maintenance. He may not be a pogonologist, but I would gladly pay to hear or read about his experience, say about the history of Van Dyke beard, or anything dating back to Assyrian braids.

Similarly, I actually had a dopamine burst about a random dude with a single subscriber leaving an essay-comment on a YouTube video how he managed to become a psychopharmaceutical "nerd" (or he wrote "geek"?) due to his experimentation of every known substance from kratom to cannabis to coffee to hallucinogens. He wrote in a scholarly manner passingly mentioning how one can become "creative" in tweaking substances to alter brain chemicals. And I knew even though he didn't have formal education, he must have oozed encyclopedic knowledge since he merely read the stuff for *kicks*!

Such niche expertise mesmerizes me. They are not too super-niche like expertise about D2 dopamine agonist receptor yielding PhD/research knowledge nor too vast where it is just about insects. If I find a beetle or a ladybug expert, I am hooked. Just the right Venn diagram lasso to be engaging enough.

Unfortunately, I have no such expertise. Sure I religiously followed cricket for the last 20 years and know some weird stuff and devoured all the Alan Watts videos gaining solemn knowledge of the oriental philosophy. And when I was not studying shell encyclopedias borrowed from the library, I read about Scops Owl, Snowy Owl, Barn Owl,

Horned Eagle Owl or whatever. But I am by no means an expert who can dazzle someone by picking any random species from the Mollusca phylum and blow someone's mind with a jaw-dropping repertoire of conchological information at length.

But I am in awe of such non-mortals. We often feel guilty about our addiction or monomania but nothing in life is eventually 'wasted'. There is always a use for some knowledge. In a Polish equivalent of the FOX TV show *Superhuman* about prodigies and mnemonists who committed vast amounts of information, there was a lady who knew all the Oscar dresses as well as a aficionado (nut!) who knew all the configuration of FIFA plays in the World Cup.

This to me is a superpower. Almost as if we are all mutants who mastered a tiny sphere of a precinct of knowledge like gods allotted certain domains to reign.

So if you 'wasted' all your life watching NFL, or getting paid dirty for auto mechanic, bingeing on Poker or gobbling nothing but pro-wrestling (like a Ken Jennings host), or poring over Bible verses and other ecumenical tomes and listening to sermons all day and night, know this my friend…

…there is a value even in that. This is precisely what makes you an expert and chosen god in your field. Life is perfect and the Universe hardly makes a mistake.

6. Accents: A Manual for Actors

So all these talk of expertise and monomania made me curious. I decided to plug in "expert of" on YouTube. Of course the searches-they-want-you-to-see revealed nothing unusual, but when I tweaked it by recent I found that almost everyone is expert on something. And I thought I had Dunning-Kruger!

Some of these expertise include:

- massage
- bed bugs
- etiquette
- bitcoin
- Yemen
- industrial coating
- aphrodisiacs
- blood stain (forensics)
- cutting
- caravan industry
- baby safety
- clothing care to last longer
- boxing
- election law
- Mali
- Indian polity

The miracle of YouTube! Of course it was the children's video "I am an expert on animal sounds" gave a thorough punch. *You gotta admire human imagination in choosing a topical theme to lay expertise upin!*

And who can forget your typical BuzzFeed and Wired "experts" weighing in on an actors' performances or special fx glitch. And expertise on accents abound.

Perhaps the best video I watched on accents was by a lady who had a natural knack for learning accents. She did an array of American accents. I especially remember the bland California one. It has been over 7 years but I distinctly recall her saying "You have to be fascinated by it".

It was during that time or even earlier I purchased Robert Blumenfeld's book. I was back to school - OCC that is - and decided to go all in on all the crazy liberal arts that included sailing, digital logic, ceramics, history of ceramics, Asian art history, epistemology, symbolic logic, anthropology and yes, theater arts. I aced some and failed a few. In Theater I did get an A. But it simply could be either my final performance was quite good (someone even said I don't have an "accent"!) or maybe because I gave a gratitude to curry favor from the professor. But either way, as one girl recalled the reason for doing it was to get "out of comfort zone" as well as a "hobby", the fact is I used this opportunity to get out of my homeostasis and give a "public speech" after my performance.

In the very first ones I didn't do too good as well. One critic pointed out: "I speak too fast!" And he was a Korean initiate who barely cracked a sentence in English! There are few as well who chimed in. And I gladly took those constructive criticisms. However, in my rendition (and interpretation) of Invisible Man I wanted to make him "gangster" (as I obviously carried tats) and give him some "weight" as well as "Serbo-Croatian, Polish or Czech accent".

The thing about college is it is...*subtle*. Very. The shades, the gradation and the degree matter. So once when the prof sparked that a good actor sticks to the script and avoids changing it giving his own spin, I didn't know if it was meant for me or others too. Or perhaps I was too stoned and weeded out in paranoia. (If not crazy shots of miniature *Spike* energy drinks.)

The fact of the matter was the acting bug really hit me that time. Heath Ledger's "Joker" was poppin' back then and I wanted to create a similar legacy whereby the character becomes larger than life and spills onto alternate reality. I wanted to give an "effect". The character needed to be a ski-masked, bank robber who "became" Invisible Man. Obviously I was way rewriting the script and taking over the camera from the director. (Later on I would equate Redmayne's "Hawking" as another perfect example of disappearance.)

The whole idea of method acting really took over me. I wanted to *become* a role. Live it. Full-fledged breath it. Animismistically bring arcane characters to life and give a makeover of a modern Hollywood version. All in visuals. In head. There was really something alluring in slumping in an armchair and disappearing into a haze of opium like Sherlock Holmes engrossed and absorbed in a case. And yes, around then that's when Downey Jr.'s rendition came out as well.

Cursory browsing of the book ignites imagination. Uzbek accent, Northern Irish accent (Belfast, Derry), Lithuanian, Prussian, Bavarian, Viennese, Burmese, Thai, Bristol, Somerset, Southwest, Valley Girl, Upstate New York...you name it! It's superspecific and you know the dude is a master of his craft. (Once I heard somewhere how certain FBI profilers can narrow down your origin down to your local region.)

The biggest takeaway from the book was just like a fingerprint every individual has her own distinct accent. I am actually irritated by commentators who nitpick polyglots or even glow how the "French accent" is just "perfect". As if everyone in France has a distinct "French accent" who just loves to r-r-r-r-r-r-r-r-oll *Pahi*.

The book comes with a CD and I listened to it often. Ipod was getting popular but I loved inserting the blue and red discs in our new car and how in a sci-fi fashion it made a *tzoooop!!* sound when it went in...

Although the book has a lot of pitch patterns and is certainly not something that can be read "word for word" but it has plethora of literary, movie and Shakespeare allusions tucked in amidst "dialect of Galician" and subsequently a sprinkle of 11th century history to make it a pleasant read and listen. This is why it gives it a strange location in my shelf space to this day. Perhaps…

Looking back these were still my fond memories. I was hooked on a nefarious substance called "Spice" but the drug vibe was palpable in sculpting and reinforcing those memories which I cherish as the life craft of kintsugi!

7. The Know-It-All

There are so many types of pasta! *Spaghettini, fedelini, vermicelloni, capellini, pici, spaghetti alla chitarra, bavettine, fettuccine, lasagne, linguine, mafalde, scialatelli, stringozzi, tagliatelle, trenette, tripoline, calamaretti, penne zita, conchiglioni, rotini, strozzapreti, gnocchi, spätzle...* and dozens more. As there are many types of *fromage*. Heck you can learn Italian or French studying just the names!

All these talk of expertise and mastery made me thus wonder. What is the limit to human knowledge? Once the instructor at *kali* (Filipino Martial Arts) declared how you can just isolate the footwork in *kali* and devote a lifetime to it. As did the mathematician Arend Heyting: "Once you are fascinated with a subject, devote a lifetime to it!" (I recall reading once.) His happened to be intuitionistic logic. Not sure I found it when I was borrowing Axiom of Choice by Horst Herrlich from UCI's Ayala Science Library after a mountainous trek and a drive of 35 minutes. I did that often. But the parking, the pilgrimage and the arduous walk from the parking lot to climb to top of the mountain to sip ambrosia of knowledge and wisdom - either from Ayala or Langson- wore off as I can easily retrieve many materials from the net.

But there is something awe-inspiring about being surrounded by thousands - literally- and thousands of books in all corners of dusty shelves from obscure thousand page monographs of some god-knows-when collogium or symposium at Berne or something all belonging to Wiley, Springer and what not. The dusty smell, the faded pages, the typewritten material.. it's a sensorium. Only thing I wish I did was down some edibles or something like speedfreak Tarski or Erdős.

You can get lost in mazes of books and who knows what nugget in a small fine print 1-sentence line you might discover! I understand the allure of research. And that's just UCI. Imagine walking down the shelves of the never-ending aislesof Library of Congress (my dream!) and you get lost in byzantine thoughts which can conjure an instant teleport to an enchanted land. And of course, there was the Library of Alexandria.

Speaking of libraries and limits to human knowledge and learning, I often wondered if one man "know it all". Apparently there are 7000 volumes of Wikipedia printed out. *Volumes* not pages. (This will sure to tick off the tree-huggers!) One dude just wanted to see what the panoramic scene looks like and the depth and vastness of it! I personally set a goal of memorizing the Oxford English Dictionary to fall flat on my face. It's impossible. Seriously, walking in water is far achievable than accessing photographic memory and blasting through all the 20,000 pages of 20 Volumes at page-a-second like Kim Peek, Will Hunting, William James Sidis, Travolta on *Phenomenon* or John Stuart Mill who once "lamented" that he cannot read as fast as he flipped pages.

Thus imagine you gain godly siddhi of photographic memory like Shas Pollak. But so what? Can you gun down all the tomes of the Library of Congress? Okay. But you don't need to read 1000 books on Nigeria to *know* about Nigeria. Sure you can narrow it down to *Britannica* or something. And that's exactly what AJ Jacobs did.

My only qualm about his experiment is that it is too forced. Just like Jesse Itzler wrote his sequel to "SEAL" for a book publication, I feel Jacobs just wanted to do it for the sake of it. There was no passion. No love. Self-proclaimed human guinea pig he is. But if you force yourself in a vice and move your neck from letter to letter, then I am sorry that is not love or fascination. That's just for the end destination of paycheck, book sign and 'work' of journalism.

Ammon Shea did the same with Oxford, but his entries were readable. Also, Jacobs seems to balance out the know-it-all part by plastering 'One Man's Humble Quest to Become the Smartest Person in the World'. I mean here you wanna be omniscient, and you had to bring humility lest you get smeared with criticism and the Internet crowd. For me it wasn't "egoistical" enough. Place it on a lap of a hip hop artist or a gangster rapper and he will make the voice and tone a *Beowulf*-masterpiece with braggadocio. If you gon' brag, might as well go all the way. Consider the entries: *jokes, cappuccino, missing links, coffee, national park*, etc. Really? You are reading *Britannica* and all you can cull out are some mundane entries? It seems he wanted to gear it to average reader and deliberately dumb it down for the general populace. I didn't get the vibe of some who has read *Britannica* cover to cover. To be fair, he starts off with unusual entries such as *a-ak, Aachen, Addled Brain Syndrome*.. but it gets worse. His humor is forced and the whole process was just too gimmicky and kitsch.

When I first got a sniff of it, I absolutely loved it. I loved the concept and wanted to get my hands on the paperback as soon as I wanted. Then at B&N I found it under "humor". The humor was wry and the whole book was bloggy to appeal to the mass market. Later I ended up watching his TED Talk which was okay and he is no doubt a funny guy, but in my not-so-humble opinion, he failed to give a full-fledged gangster vibe after going 'around-the-world'. The book was too 'Simp' for me. The thing is I *wanted* to love it.

Later I would still pick it up from that used book store from Buena Park Mall for 2 or 3 bucks, instead of that $19.99 price, because this is no doubt a tremendous human achievement and deserves to be in anyone's book shelf. Consider this encomium from a website called 80000hours.org:

He's also spent months saying whatever was on his mind, tried to become the healthiest person in the world, read 33,000 pages of facts, spent a year following the Bible literally, thanked everyone involved in making his morning cup of coffee, and tried to figure out how to do the most good. His next book will ask: if we reframe global problems as puzzles, would the world be a better place?

I do think he is a genius despite the pedestrian writing style. I feel people like him, Jesse Itzler and others have this 'notion' on what a baseline authors' voice should be and they are too afraid of injecting their own strong inner personality for fear of alienation.

Consider this from *The Red-Headed League* of Doyle where Sherlock Holmes offers a pearl of wisdom:

> "Grave enough!" said Mr. Jabez Wilson. "Why, I have lost four pound a week."

> "As far as you are personally concerned," remarked Holmes, "I do not see that you have any grievance against this extraordinary league. On the contrary, you are, as I understand, richer by some £30, to say nothing of the minute knowledge which you have gained on every subject which comes under the letter A. You have lost nothing by them."

No doubt the respect is there. But it would have been stronger had he a more *ex cathedra* authoritative vibe as Holmes.